The Developmentally Appropriate Inclusive Classroom in Early Education

TABLE OF CONTENTS

This table of contents is arranged with one chapter outlined per page so that an overhead transparency may be made of each chapter to serve as a graphic organizer for the lecture and class discussion.

PART 1

CHAPTER 1

Introduction

- Developmentally Appropriate Curriculum and Practice

- Guidelines for Developmentally Appropriate Practice

- How Children Learn

- Inclusion

- The Children in an Inclusive Classroom

- The Teachers in an Inclusive Classroom

CHAPTER 2

Integrated Thematic Play and Curriculum

- Overview of Thematic Approach

- Definition of Integrated Curriculum

- Curriculum to Accommodate All Children

- Child Populations and Child Age Considerations

- Benefits of the Integrated Curriculum Approach

- Classroom Discipline and Management

CHAPTER 3

Developing the Integrated Curriculum

- Space

- Furniture and Equipment

- Materials and Books

- Schedule and Routine

- Facilitation of Activity

PART 2
CHAPTER 4

Planning the Integrated Curriculum

- The Early Childhood Educator as the Key to the Success of this Approach
- What are the Steps To Be Followed when Planning an Integrated Curriculum
- Pitfalls and Problems of Child-Centered Planning
- Peers as Nurturers and Facilitators
- Supporting the Development of All Children
- Language and Literacy Development
- Social Development
- Physical Development
- Cognitive Development: Thinking and Problem-solving Skills
- Overview of Appropriate Activity Areas
- Meet the Children

CHAPTER 5

Art

- Importance of Art Activities for Development

- Objectives of Art Activities for Children With and Without Disabilities

- Developmentally Appropriate Activities and Materials

- Modification of Materials or Activities to Include Children with Special Needs

- Case Studies Describing Modifications

Chapter 6

Sensory

- Importance of Sensory Activities for Development

- Objectives of Sensory Activities

- Developmentally Appropriate Activities and Materials With and Without Disabilities

- Modification of Materials or Activities to Include Children with Special Needs

- Case Studies Describing Modifications

CHAPTER 7

Manipulatives and Small Blocks

- Importance of Manipulative and Small Block Activities for Development

- Objectives of Manipulative Activities

- Objectives of Small Block Activities

- Developmentally Appropriate Activities and Manipulative Materials

- Modification of Materials or Activities to Include Children with Special Needs

- Case Studies Describing Modifications

CHAPTER 8

Dramatic Play in the Large Blocks and Housekeeping Corners

- Importance of Dramatic Play Activities for Development

- Objectives of Dramatic Play Activities

- Developmentally Appropriate Activities and Materials

- Modifications of Materials or Activities to Include Children with Special Needs

- Case Studies Describing Modifications

CHAPTER 9

Large Motor Development

- Importance of Large Motor Activities for Development

- Objectives of Large Motor Activities

- Developmentally Appropriate Activities and Materials

- Modification of Materials or Activities to Include Children with Special Needs

- Case Studies Describing Modifications

CHAPTER 10

Music and Movement

- Importance of Music and Movement Activities for Development

- Objectives of Music and Movement Activities

- Developmentally Appropriate Activities and Materials

- Modification of Materials or Activities to Include Children with Special Needs

- Case Studies Describing Modifications

CHAPTER 11

Language and Literacy

- Importance of Language and Literacy Activities for Development

- Objectives of Language and Literacy Activities

- Developmentally Appropriate Activities and Materials

- Modification of Materials or Activities to Include Children with Special Needs

- Case Studies Describing Modifications

CHAPTER 12

Sample Integrated Themes

- Developed Integrated Theme
- Guidelines for General Modifications of Activities
- Resource of Ideas for Development of a Theme
- Theme: Processes—How Things Work, Move, and Change
- Resource of Ideas for Theme: Homes
- Ideas for Other Developmentally Appropriate Themes
- Integrating the IEP or IFSP into Classroom Activities
- Bridging Classroom Curriculum to Home

PART 3
CHAPTER 13

Parents and Families

- Role of the Parent in the Development of the Child
- Influence of Home on the Development of a Child
- Factors that Might Interfere with Home and School Involvement
- What Teachers Gain from Parent-Teacher Relationships
- What Parents Gain from Parent-Teacher Relationships
- Forging the Relationship
- Barriers to Effective Parent-Teacher Relationships
- Partnerships with Consultants and Specialists
- Consultation
- Collaboration
- Working with Teachers and Specialists to Plan for Transitions

CHAPTER 14

Specialists as Members of the Team

- Roles of Various Support Specialists
- Understanding the Classroom Culture
  How Does Therapy Fit?
- Team Approaches to Service Delivery
- Support Specialists in the Assessment Role
- Support Specialists in the Consultant Role
- The Paraprofessional in the Inclusive Classroom
- Managing and Coordinating Service Delivery
- Partnerships with Support Specialists and Consultant
- Collaboration
- Support Specialists within Community Early Childhood Programs
- Communication with Parents
- The Early Childhood Teacher as Collaborator and Communicator
- Working with Families in Planning for Transitions

CHAPTER 15

Observation and Assessment

- Observation as Assessment in Inclusive Developmentally Appropriate Settings
- Observation Techniques
- Observation as Assessment in Different Activity Areas
- Preserving and Compiling Information on Children
- Ethics of "Assessment"
- What is Assessment?
- Why Must Teachers Assess?
- When Do Teachers Assess?
- How Do Teachers Assess?
- What Happens to Assessments?

DISCUSSION QUESTIONS

At the end of each of the chapters in this book, with the exception of Chapter 12, there are several discussion questions designed to stimulate the student to focus on critical issues or potential problems. Many of the questions are presented in an applied manner and require that the student respond to issues or problems in a practical manner. Other questions suggest that the student engage in discussion with a peer.

While experiential situations may be different for each group of individuals using this text, there may be many similarities in terms of the types of responses desired for each question. What follows is a listing of each of the discussion questions found in the chapters. After each question are some possible highlights of responses to each of the questions. These highlights are by no means an exhaustive list of what should be contained in each response, but rather a sense of the direction each question could take.

CHAPTER 1
Introduction

1) Problem: The mother of a young boy shared a concern with a guest speaker after a parent night in a community preschool. The father of the child was in the military and was away for long periods of time. The child developed an interest in and seemed to want to own a doll. The father was set against it and told the mother she was never to get him a doll. The mother went along with the directive for a period of time, but finally gave in because the child seemed to miss his father so much when he was away. The mother related that she told the child he could not play with the doll or even show the doll to the father when he was at home. When the father was home, the doll stayed in the closet. The mother wondered if she had created a new problem while attempting to deal with an existing one.

What would you say to this mother? What could you suggest to her that she do to make the situation less confusing for the child?

- talk to the mother about trust
- healthy emotional development requires consistency
- living within two behavioral conditions—father home, father away could be very confusing and frustrating for the child
- to reduce confusion for the child, the mother should try to educate the father as to the appropriateness of the child having a doll
- the mother could attempt to speak to the child trying to explain why the father feels the way he does (lack of experience with dolls, non-sexist toys, etc.)

2) Problem: You are a new teacher in an old established early childhood program. You have very strong ideas about the infusion of an anti-bias approach into the curriculum. Once you begin to settle into the job, you realize that the program director and the teachers have an established curriculum that identifies weekly themes that are offered in a set sequence. They have followed this curriculum for many years. How will you handle this situation?

- share previous experiences with other staff
- share current resources supporting the infusion of an anti-bias approach
- introduce anti-bias activities and materials within what already exists in the program to attempt some change into the curriculum

3) Problem: You respond to a telephone inquiry concerning the early childhood program in which you work. The family making the inquiry wants to know the philosophy of the program. You discuss developmentally appropriate curriculum and practice and indicate that the program includes children with disabilities. The parent seems uncomfortable with this information. What will you say in response to this parent?
- attempt to confirm information the parent is most concerned about
- find out if the parent understands that a program that includes children with disabilities is a program that is concerned about the individual development of each individual child
- invite the parent to visit to see how the program works
- invite the parent to speak to parents whose children have already completed the program

4) Describe two situations you have observed in which activities could have been presented in a manner making them more accessible and developmentally appropriate for all children in the class.
- look for suggestions in modifications of materials
- look for suggestions in modifications of presentation
- look for suggestions in modifications of activity location

5) Think about a situation in which you worked with a child or observed a child who was experiencing stress. What did you do or could you have done to alleviate the stress?
- teach the child how to relax (deep breaths, count slowly)
- redirect the child to a less stressful activity or situation
- talk to the child about alternative responses to the situation

6) Friends of yours ask for your advice about the selection of toys for their children for birthday gifts. Their children are 4, 6, and 8 years old. What suggestions will you give them, and what can you tell them about the developmental importance and appropriateness of the items you suggest?
- look for suggestions of non-sexist books, dolls, manipulatives, and games
- look for suggestions of open-ended materials that can be used over time
- look for suggestions for toys that can be used both individually or with another one or more children
- look for suggestions for materials that provide for creative outlets
- look for suggestions for materials that interface with other materials or equipment to extend play

CHAPTER 2
Integrated Thematic Play and Curriculum

1) Problem: A grandparent brings a grandchild to school and with the child holding on to her hand, informs you that the only way the grandchild in her care is going to behave for you is if you hit the child. The grandparent gives you permission to do it. What can you say to this person and to the child to set a different tone?

- speak to the importance of encouraging self-control when caring for children
- speak to your approach of expecting age appropriate behavior and providing consequences that are logical to the situation

2) Problem: You are required to visit a classroom to make an observation. You call the number of a teacher that someone in your neighborhood has given you. Since you do not know anything about the school the teacher works in, you ask for some information about the class. The teacher tells you that it is a kindergarten class that has twenty-four children who are all on different levels. Three of the children have language problems and two of them are children with mild physical disabilities. The teacher also informs you that in this classroom all children are treated the same way. There is no special treatment. Everyone is expected to accomplish the same work in the same manner, and behave according to the rules of the classroom. You decide to reflect on the information given to you over the phone before you make an appointment to visit. What are your thoughts about what you heard? Will you schedule a visit?
- is it realistic to expect that children who operate at different levels in the same class will be able to complete the same work?
- is it realistic to have children with disabilities working under the same expectations as children without disabilities?

3) The parents of a child in the first grade are concerned because the child does not have any workbooks or worksheets to do. The parents ask you what you think about this since they know that you are studying early childhood education. What will you tell them? What will you tell them to look for instead of looking for workbooks and worksheets?
- speak to them about the importance of hands-on learning versus the more traditional paper and pencil approach to learning
- tell them to look for lots of books, manipulatives, open ended materials and activities

4) Think back to your early years in school. What are your memories of classroom activities? Why do you remember them? Who are the people you most remember? Why do you remember them?
- encourage students to think about whether there were manipulative art and dramatic play activities
- encourage discussion about teachers, aides, parents, administrators, peers

5) You have been given an assignment that requires you to brainstorm ideas for two themes appropriate for young children with another person in your class. You set a date to get together and the other person indicates that she thinks it would be easier to choose at least one holiday, such as Thanksgiving as a theme. You are not comfortable with the idea. Discuss what you would say to your classmate when you get together. What other themes could you suggest as alternatives and why?

- encourage suggestion of themes that involve more on-going experiences that children have rather than themes that relate to once a year events
- encourage your co-planner to think about the experiences children have that provide them with rich language and hands-on learning

6) Discuss the ways in which you could find out what interested the children in your class. Once you had that information, what would it allow you to do?
- look for emphasis on observation of children at play
- listen to the conversations children have with each other and with adults
- once you know what children are interested in, you can plan activities in those areas

CHAPTER 3
Developing the Integrated Curriculum

1) After visiting two different early childhood programs, compare and contrast these programs for aspects of developmental appropriateness. Think about the issues of space, materials, furniture and equipment, schedule and routine and the facilitation of activity.
- look to make sure that students understand that factors in early childhood programs can be different and still be developmentally appropriate
- look for the similarities as well as differences between the programs

2) Problem: You have been invited to visit a site that may possibly be developed into some kind of early childhood program. The site is a former factory location. What concern will you bring to the site when you visit that relate to the creation of safe, developmentally appropriate programs.
- the space needs to be safe and healthy
- the space needs to be accessible
- the space needs to be large enough to allow children to engage in the activities designed for the space
- the space will be adequate to accommodate the storage of materials not used every day

3) You are asked to help develop a list of materials that are absolutely necessary to start a mixed-age preschool program. The list should contain justifications for each of the items. The budget is limited.
- manipulatives, books, dramatic play materials, discovery oriented materials, sensory materials, art materials

4) What are some of the benefits of collaboration between early childhood teachers? Discuss both the pros and cons.
- better use of space
- sharing of materials and equipment
- sharing in the design and implementation of activities
- one teacher can be very forceful and take the lead at all times
- one teacher can take a back seat to another and let the teacher lead

5) Problem: You are a teacher in an early childhood program that supports the guidelines of developmentally appropriate practice. You have the chance to observe a potential teacher in your classroom. The teacher candidate has been asked to participate during the free choice of planned activity period of the day. What will you look for as indicators of appropriateness of this candidate and why?

- teacher acting as facilitator of activity
- teacher serving as language model
- teacher supports choices and decision making
- teacher engages in activity with children

6) Discuss the possible adaptations most environments will need to make to accommodate children with disabilities.
- widen pathways between activities and areas
- ramps
- opportunities for crossing safely from one area to another
- space should not be too cluttered

CHAPTER 4
Planning the Integrated Curriculum

1) Discuss the role of the early childhood teacher with regard to the development and implementation of integrated thematic curriculum.
- teachers are the ones who spend considerable time with children; they know a lot about individual children in their classes
- teachers are the ones who implement curriculum so they should be able to develop what makes sense for the children in the class within the guidelines of what is both age and individually appropriate

2) Problem: You have a small classroom. You want to provide a variety of activity areas but have limited space. Brainstorm ways to provide a variety of activity areas within the space constraints you have.
- use surface space as well as floor space
- rotate the types of activity areas you make available within the day and/or from day to day

3) Problem: You are planning to have a parent meeting soon. It is the first one of the year. You want the program to inform parents about the integrated curriculum approach. What are the key elements you will stress in order to have parents understand what goes on in your classroom on a daily basis.
- integrated curriculum is thematically organized
- integrated curriculum makes logical connections for children so they are not learning bits of information in isolation
- integrated curriculum is designed to meet the needs of the children in the classroom

4) Problem: You observe a child being very responsive to a child with disabilities. The responsive child is eager to help and seems to have a sense of appropriate helping. How can you nurture the situation to the benefit of both children?
- suggest and/or demonstrate helping and nurturing behaviors that are not burdensome to the child who wants to help
- guide the child to learn how to help without being overbearing

- help the child who wants to nurture to see that too much nurturing may prevent the child with disabilities from being motivated to do things independently

5) Problem: A salesperson calls and attempts to sell you a language development kit that contains books, puppets, picture cards and a teacher's manual. What is your response to this salesperson? Why?
- help students to think about the pros and cons of "kits" versus teacher developed curriculum
- discuss the implementation of curriculum designed by someone who does not know the children in the individual class in which the curriculum is to be implemented
- the materials and activities in the "kit" may be too basic or too advanced for the children in the individual class

6) Is it vital to address all areas of development within the early childhood years? Is it appropriate to develop an early childhood program that specializes on one or more areas? Why or why not?
- the early childhood years are the time to expose children to a variety of experiences; they are curious and receptive; it is the time to attend to the whole child
- children become "departmentalized" soon enough and should not be overly focused within one or two aspects of development at an early age

CHAPTER 5
Art

1) Discuss the benefits of open-ended art activities for the development of young children.
- children benefit from exploration of art materials; when there is a model for a child to follow or an end product displayed that a child feels he/she must reproduce, the child may become inhibited in artistic expression
- children learn about color, design, space, beauty and expression when activities are open-ended
- children explore different media without criticism
- children find freedom in the flexibility and lack of "exactness" of open-ended activity

2) Collect samples of art work over a period of time. Compare the samples looking at the use of color, shape, the area of the paper used, the degree of representation identified. Discuss your findings with another student who has completed the same collection process.
- look for discussion about possible age differences in the art collected
- look for discussion about the effect of experience over time
- look for discussion about the possible differences in the art produced between boys and girls

3) Problem: You read an article in the local newspaper that highlights an early childhood teacher who speaks to the importance of coloring within the lines. Prepare a response to the article to be sent in the form of a letter to the editor.
- speak to the confining nature of emphasis on coloring in the lines
- discuss the fact that coloring within the lines is a motor skill and not an artistic behavior
- discuss developmental differences in children

4) Problem: A child is ready to be picked up from your kindergarten class. The child is holding a lunchbox and carrying three pieces of art work completed recently. When the parent leaves with the child, you notice that the parent takes the art work and deposits it in the trash can near the door to the classroom. What can you do in the future to prevent this situation from happening again?
- create a place in the room for children to display art and encourage that child to keep art work at school
- prepare information for parents about the importance of and nature of art in the early childhood years

5) Select one of the child cases in this chapter. Brainstorm activities you think would be appropriate for the child you choose. Identify any modifications you think would be required in order for the child to carry out the activity.
- look for students to be sensitive to the individual needs of children with the varying disabilities indicated in the cases
- look for creative brainstorming and reflection on what is known and not known about the children

6) Think back to you early school years. List the art activities you remember doing. Compare your list with that of another student in your class.
- look to see if students in the class experienced product versus process art
- look to see if students experienced collaborative projects
- look to see if students experienced art as part of units of study and/or as independent free activity

CHAPTER 6
Sensory

1) Problem: You are a new first grade teacher in a school where teachers are beginning to embrace the developmentally appropriate approach to planning environments for young children. You have volunteered to help the early childhood teachers develop sensory areas and activities for their classrooms. What will you suggest as appropriate for the younger and older children?
- look for responses showing concern for safety within the area
- basic sensory experiences for the younger, less experienced children
- sensory materials with accessories for older children
- as language skills and observations skills develop, create opportunities to make predictions
- introduce dramatic play opportunities after children have had basic experiences with a variety of sensory materials

2) Get together with a classmate and brainstorm ideas for varying experiences with sand that could relate to a specific theme of your choice.
- look for ideas that evidence sensitivity to the range of possible variations on sand play that can be introduced to children across the early childhood age span
- look for suggestions that can relate to thematic study

3) Develop a column for a parent newsletter that explains the importance of sensory experiences for children. Include a few suggestions for parents to implement in the home.
- include information about the opportunities for:

- comparing and contrasting
- measuring
- learning about characteristics and properties of materials
- children learn from repeated explorations
- sensory experiences encourage language, motor, and conceptual development

4) Problem: The person who maintains the building in which you teach voices concern about the "mess" that your sensory activities create. Brainstorm ideas of how the activities can be cleaned up by the children and adults in the room so the maintainer will be content and the materials will not attract insects, etc. to your room.
- children participate in the clean up using shovels and pails to empty the container
- children use dust broom and dust pan to clean floor
- children use dust buster or vacuum to clean up
- an element of dramatic play is introduced to the cleaning process
- children are given spray bottles with water and sponges to clean with

5) Problem: You have included in your room a child with physical disabilities who is always exceptionally clean and beautifully dressed. While your intent is not to cause the child to get dirty, you wish to have the child engage in sensory activities to the fullest potential of the child. What can you do to communicate your intent to the parents and prevent the child from becoming covered with whatever substance the child will use in the sensory area?
- encourage the parents to think of dressing the child to be able to participate in whatever activities are available
- point out the need to have the child and the teachers feel comfortable with participation without worrying about ruining clothing
- look for alternatives to traditional smocks for children with disabilities who require the use of adaptive equipment

6) Think about how sensory exploration relates to the world of work. Discuss with a classmate the similarities between these activities and the many careers individuals have in which they work with the same substances on a regular basis.
- look for suggestions of traditional and non-traditional careers of persons who work with water, sand, fabric, grain, soil, dough, paper, spices, wood, or sandpaper

CHAPTER 7
Manipulatives and Small Blocks

1) Select two manipulatives from an early childhood catalogue. Compare and contrast them noting their size, color, the material it is made from, the number of pieces in the manipulative, the cost and the flexibility with which the manipulative may be used with a variety of children. Discuss the results of your comparison with a classmate.
- see if students identify more than one way to use each of the manipulative materials selected from the catalogue
- see if students identify varying uses of the manipulatives contingent on age and/or ability of children

2) Problem: A parent informs you that the first thing her child talks about each day after school is what was created with the manipulatives made available to the children that day. The parent indicated that they do not have any of these kinds of materials at home. It appears that the mother would like to be able to provide this type of experience for the child at home. What can you suggest to the mother that would be inexpensive, safe and developmentally appropriate for the child to use?
- encourage the mother to save many containers of different sizes and shapes for stacking and building
- encourage the mother to collect interesting magazine pictures, mount them on cardboard, and cut them into puzzle pieces
- sequence cards can be created with comics and advertisements
- pattern cards can be made with stickers that come with advertisements
- save beads, spools, and buttons for matching and patterning activities

3) Problem: A child always wants to use certain manipulatives independently and you are attempting to build in a socialization component for the use of these manipulatives. What can you do to move the child more in your desired direction without having the child leave the area entirely?
- divide the manipulatives into two or more containers so that children will need to ask each other for specific pieces
- provide a large surface on which to use the manipulatives that can accommodate two or more children who might initially use different areas of the surface and move more toward each other over time

4) Problem: A child in your class, if allowed, will remain working with manipulatives or blocks during the entire play period. How can you arrange the environment to interest the child in other areas so the child will be able to take advantage of a broader range of experiences?
- develop a system of children starting the day in a different area every few days
- have children "punch in" to different activity areas as the participate in activities
- create buddy relationships for children who are reluctant to try other areas
- make the manipulatives available later in the day so that children will try new areas earlier in the day

5) Prepare information concerning the use of blocks and manipulatives for volunteers who work in your classroom on a regular basis. This information should be general enough to serve the purpose for the entire year but specific enough to answer most questions that these people might have.
- look for information about some of the benefits of manipulative and small blocks for early childhood development
- point out the long term effects these experiences have on academic development
- emphasize that technology does not replace the need for manipulative and blocks experience

6) Problem: A child builds a complex structure with the small blocks. The child worked on the structure during the entire play period. When it is time to clean up, the child asks if the structure may remain standing so that his mother may see it at the end of the day and so that he may play with it and add to it the next day. What will you say to the child and why?
- you could tell the child you will photograph the structure and share the photo with the mother, but that the structure must be cleaned up so the space can be used for other activity or by other people

• you could put partitions around the structure so save it for the mother to see with the provision that the child needs to clean it up after the mother looks at it

CHAPTER 8
Dramatic Play in the Large Blocks and Housekeeping Corners

1) Problem: There are no dramatic play materials in your kindergarten classroom which is one of four rooms to be undergoing a transformation from academic focus to developmentally appropriate focus. How will you acquire what you wish to have in the room? Is there any way you may work cooperatively with the other teachers?
   • ask parents for donations of clothing, utensils, floral arrangements, tolls, broken small appliances, etc.
   • ask senior citizens groups for donations of the above
   • frequent tag sales

2) Think about the themes you used to play when you were a young child. What do you think influenced those themes? What themes do you observe children playing when the theme is of their own choice? What do you think motivates those choices of theme?
   • media influences—TV, radio, movies, videos
   • discuss media influences—positive and negative
   • discuss trendy toys as influences
   • discuss role of older siblings as influence

3) Problem: You observe children playing a theme you think has potential to become negative in terms of scaring some children, excluding some children, and becoming too loud and rowdy for indoor play. What will your response as teacher, facilitator, and overall classroom "manager" be to the situation? Why?
   • look for ideas relating to gentle intervention and reorientation of play that appears to be heading in a negative direction
   • look for ideas indicating that the adult take on a role within the play that can redirect the play without the adult having to take on the role of prohibitor
   • look for ideas to create signs that will prohibit the play without the adult having to do it
   • consider having a "town meeting" to discuss the turn of events

4) Problem: At the start of the school year, the parents of your first grade students seemed to be supportive of the children playing in the classroom. Now it is close to mid-year and several of the parents have asked when the children will stop playing and begin doing some real work. What will you say to these parents to explain the reason the children are playing and what it is that they are learning through play. Discuss the role of play in:
   • socialization
   • language development
   • application of knowledge
   • cognitive development
   • reading skills
   • math skills

5) With a classmate, brainstorm some ideas for dramatic play activities appropriate for an integrated theme you mutually select. Think about the materials you would like to have to support the dramatic play.
- look for ideas from students that indicate that the students have engaged in collective brainstorming resulting in a multitude of ideas
- look for ideas from students that go beyond the basics
- look for ideas for materials that show "stretching"

6) Problem: You observe over a period of time that there is a child with disabilities in your class who engages in dramatic play for very brief periods of time. This is a concern you wish to address. What ideas do you have to involve the child in more sustained play?
- look for ideas which indicate brainstorming of alternate roles children may play
- look for ideas which indicate reorganization of the environment to incorporate the child with disabilities
- practice appropriate play behaviors with the child with disabilities so that the child will develop stronger skills necessary to be used in dramatic play

CHAPTER 9
Large Motor Development

1) Problem: The weather prevents being able to go outdoors for days on end. With a classmate brainstorm what you can do to substitute for this activity thinking about variety and appropriateness.
- look for ideas that suggest creating a time during the day for exercise of some sort that does not require considerable space
- look for ideas that involve children in stretching and bending that may be done in more confined areas
- look for ideas for dramatic play that use more large motor activity

2) Parents of a child in your classroom inform you that they are signing their child up for two sports teams as well as gymnastics lessons. They want to know what you think of all this wonderful activity. What will your response to them be? Why?
- look for discussion pro and con relative to the merits of organized sports and lessons for young children
- look for support for each of these statements regardless of whether the statement is pro or con

3) Observe one child during play activities and list all the physical actions you observe the child engage in during that time. Compare your list with the list of a classmate comparing activities present during the observation, the number of children in the program, and the ages of the children observed. Look for information regarding:
- range of motion
- repetitive motions
- how much of the time children are physically active during play of all types

4) Problem: A child in your room appears to fall for no apparent reason. When the path is clear, with no materials equipment or furniture in the way, the child occasionally hits the floor making contact on the knees. The knees are consistently bruised. What can you do to determine the cause of the problem? What modifications might be made to program and environment to remedy the situation?

- look for ideas to assess movement ability through regular school activities
- look for concerns about the visual ability of the child
- look for ideas to develop activities for the child that would practice and regulate gait and posture

5) Problem: A child in your room is never observed using the climbing apparatus available in the playground. What resources do you have to encourage the child to participate?
- look for ideas to create dramatic play outdoors that involves the use of the outdoor climbing equipment
- look to develop a relationship between that child and a child who can nurture, encourage, and demonstrate the use of the equipment
- look for discussion about the role of the teacher in praising and motivating the use of something new

6) Problem: There is a child with disabilities in your class who does not seem to understand or want to heed your message about the danger of jumping down stairs. What can you do to create a safer situation for the child without making the child fearful of other physical activity?
- look for suggestions relating to safe practice of using the stairs
- look for suggestions of limit setting by the adults in the room

CHAPTER 10
Music and Movement

1) Problem: Teachers in your school get together to plan thematic integrated curriculum. When they plan they brainstorm ideas for books, art activities, dramatic play, and sensory/science opportunities. You are new to the team and want to suggest that planning for music and movement should be an integral part of the planning. What can you offer to the team to make this planning happen?
- offer to do the "leg work" for the team and come in with songs, chants, fingerplays, appropriate music and suggestions for movement activity to support the objectives of the integrated unit

2) Problem: Space is a problem in your classroom. You want to include movement activities in your program but feel you do not have the space. What can you do to create an atmosphere that will promote movement activities? What can you do to rearrange the physical space in the classroom?
- move furniture to the sides of the room in order to make room in the center of the room for movement
- have children stand in place and engage in upper torso movement activities
- have children sit on the floor for circle time and engage in upper torso body movement
- have a few children do movement activity at a time so less space is needed

3) You do not know many songs and feel the need to build your repertoire. How will you go about learning more songs and develop them into a workable collection that you can use in planning integrated curriculum. Get together with a classmate to share song collections.
- go to the library to listen to and borrow records and tapes
- find a teacher resource center and borrow song tapes

- take a Music for Young Children course
- visit the library and look through multicultural song books, if you do not read music, find someone who can play and tape the songs for you

4) Problem: There are a few children in your class with low level language ability. You notice that these children have a strong interest in music and movement activities. How will you work within the framework of music and movement to enhance the language level of these children.
- use musical games that are language based
- being part of the music circle while participating in the motions of songs encourages language and may serve as the key to unlocking language
- use expandable songs to encourage at least one word language participation

5) Brainstorm resources for music and movement in your community that are appropriate for young children. Discuss these findings with a classmate.
- look for suggestions that include community music groups as well as community movement and dance groups
- look for suggestions from retired musicians or dancers who would like to share their enthusiasm with young children
- look for suggestions of high school and college students who are able to work with young children in an intern capacity

6) Problem: A child in your class is very withdrawn. The child has not connected with any of the other children in the room but has connected with you. Is there any way you think that music and movement activities might help the child to become less withdrawn? Develop a plan for facilitating this happening. Discuss the plan with a classmate.
- music and movement activities can be a means of encouraging children to be in closer proximity to peers
- being even minimally part of music and movement activities builds self-concept and brings the child closer to social interaction
- music activity can encourage language that can be used in social situations
- do not force the child to participate in any activity
- try to use puppets to encourage participation in activity

CHAPTER 11
Language and Literacy

1) Develop a list of words for activities and objects commonly used during the course of a morning at school. Think of ways to explain or demonstrate the definitions of those words to children so all children will be able to understand regardless of their language level.
- use actual photos of the areas to identify what the labels for the areas mean
- use picture cards to help children plan their activities
- use pictures and words to label materials
- introduce activities be role playing specific behaviors during group times

2) Discuss the role of the teacher in the integrated curriculum with regard to language development and enhancement. Specify behaviors a teacher should engage in to facilitate language while children are engaged in activity.
- teacher needs to serve as a language model, model without overwhelming a child with too many words
- teacher needs to be a good listener, active listening reflects back to children and offers suggestions of appropriate words to label objects and describe actions and activities
- have fun with words during activities
- try to connect the language of individual children to build conversation during activity if appropriate

3) Prepare information to share with parents about the importance of reading to children as a strong foundation for language and literacy. With this information include some ideas for books, alternative materials, and activities to encourage literacy at home.
- encourage parents to see that routine home activities such as making lists, checking food ads, clipping coupons, reading labels add to literacy development
- encourage parents to read to children or provide books on tape that can be shared with the whole family
- listen to literature radio programs together
- provide paper and pencils for children to use
- encourage children to "read" to the family

4) Problem: A child in your class tends to be very quiet. When the child speaks, the child uses very appropriate language. The teachers are pleased with the progress to date. One day, the child's mother comes to school and informs the teachers that she is concerned about the bad words the child has been using at home. She is quiet and shy herself and does not feel comfortable sharing the words of concern with the teachers. The teachers put their heads together to brainstorm what the child might be saying considering all the "richness" of possibilities that a child could learn from in the classroom. When the teachers talk to the mother and express their shared concern about the level of discomfort the mother feels, she tells the teachers that the child was calling them "stupid" at home. The teachers were relieved that the word of concern was not stronger but realize that the mother has a valid concern and needs assistance with the elimination of language that is distasteful to the family as well as support for her feelings. What can you say to the mother to help her and to validate her feelings? What can you do at school to help with the problem?
- indicate that while she does not like the language the child used, children do learn language from their peers, even negative language
- suggest that while she should be concerned, showing too much concern about the words may cause the child to be too interested in using them again
- respect the values the mother is attempting to impart to her child
- show your support by telling the mother that you will talk to the children about good words and bad words

5) Problem: A parent comes to you to express concern over the fact that the children in the school do not learn how to spell. When the parent went to school, learning ten spelling words per week was an important part of the curriculum. What will you tell the parent to explain why this is the not the focal point of the curriculum in your school?

- explain that when the focus is on correct spelling, children lose the spontaneity in writing
- explain that invented spelling is understood by the child doing the writing and encourages increased productivity in writing
- explain to the parent that it is more important to establish writing first and then command attention to correct spelling later on

6) Problem: A child comes to your kindergarten class without any preschool experience. The child is the appropriate chronological age for school but as you get to know the child, it appears that the child is not at the same age developmentally. You are concerned about the child's language level and feel the need to develop a plan of action to enhance the language level of the child. Your plan should include individualized attention, group activities as well as home activities.
- special attention should be given to the child on a one-to-one basis in order to provide more language modeling and to ensure that someone listens to the language the child produces everyday
- find specific roles for the child in group activities such as placing a flannel board piece during the telling of a story, or adding a word during the singing of a song
- have the child pass out cups at snack time
- make suggestions to the parents to encourage having the child answer the phone, suggest foods for mealtimes, choose books to be read at home.

CHAPTER 12

Sample Integrated Themes

Although there are no discussion questions for this chapter, discussions may be encouraged concerning the variety of activities contained within the chapter themes. Variations to these activities may be suggested.

CHAPTER 13

Parents and Families

1) Describe one or more situations when you observed a teacher facilitated parent involvement when it appeared that the parent was not going to easily become part of the group or program.
- look for observations about parent reluctance to share in group discussions but once the group was over, several of the parents wanted individual attention from the teacher
- look for observations about parent activity sessions where the parents may have been shy to use the materials set out for them to explore
- look for situations when parents attended a meeting but sat so far away from the other parents that the distance appeared to make other feel uncomfortable

2) Problem: You sent home two newsletters containing important information about upcoming events, permission slips required, etc. One particular child assures you that the newsletters have been handed over to the parents. You have received nothing back from them. You are concerned

about the level of involvement of this family and want to contact them. Try to think of all the means possible to establish communication with these parents taking into account reasons why the parents have not responded to date.
- parents may not be able to read—call to "remind" them of the contents of the newsletters without prying into their reading ability
- English may not be the language of the parent—try to have another parent who is bilingual make the "reminder" call
- parents may be out of town and the person caring for the child does not want to take certain responsibilities, a call to the home will validate that information
- the parent may have overwhelming responsibilities with work, family, and extended family issues, when the call is made, sensitivity should prevail

3) Design a plan for establishing communication with parents of children in your classroom. In your plan, include the rationale for each form of and occasion for communication over the school year. Will the approach change over time? Why?
- look for suggestions of varying written forms of communication: newsletters, calendars, copies of child generated language experience stories, recipes of foods prepared with the children
- look for suggestions using videotapes made during the course of regular daily routines that could go home with different families at different times
- phone calls
- audiotapes made during group discussions

4) Problem: The parent of a child in your class is challenging you about what the parent perceives to be "a lack of academics" in the program. You have presented all the parents with written information about the developmentally appropriate approach to planning and implementing curriculum. You have invited the parent to visit the classroom. The parent visited once when the children acted out a story they had been reading. The parent seems to spend considerable time talking to other parents at arrival and dismissal times. What can you do to help this parent understand the process that is taking place in the classroom and the importance of the process?
- you can give this parent literature to read that explains the role of discovery learning for young children
- suggest that the parent speak to parents of older children who have experienced this type of learning already
- research the availability of parent focused videos concerning developmentally appropriate practice
- encourage the parent to talk to the child about activities and experience the child has at school in an open-ended manner

5) Your goal for the year is to have 100% parent participation. You are not concerned about the nature of the participation but you want each parent or family representative to be involved in something. Create a "menu" of opportunities for parents that reflects a variety of opportunities building on a variety of interests and skills.
- provide materials
- type newsletters
- assist with classroom activities
- collect "junk" for the classroom

- build furniture or equipment
- put together class book and individual books
- attend meetings
- encourage others to attend meetings
- research possible field trips
- make arrangements for field trips

6) You plan to accompany a family to a PPT meeting for their child. The focus of the meeting is planning for transition to first grade. The family is uneasy about the move to what they perceive to be a more academically demanding environment. What can you do to help them ahead of time to prepare for the meeting so that they will feel more comfortable in their role? What can you do at the meeting to make sure the parents hear what they need to hear?
- review the progress the child made during the year
- review the current procedures and any therapies in place for the child
- identify the needs of the child still unmet
- discuss the pros and cons of the present and previous classrooms
- discuss ideas for the ideal first grade classroom
- discuss ideas for what needs to be in place to make a smoother transition for the child
- at the meeting take notes, listen, and reflect the discussion
- keep track of the responses to the issues identified prior to the PPT date

CHAPTER 14
Specialists as Members of the Team

1) Develop an approach to integrating specialists into an inclusive classroom. Indicate the steps you would take to explain your program and make the specialists feel as comfortable as possible.
- provide them with any written materials available concerning the philosophy of the classroom program
- set aside time to give them a tour of the classroom
- provide updates about the program you follow through the sharing of newsletters, etc.
- regularly greet these people as welcome additions to your classroom rather than see them as interruptions, they provide valuable service to the children with disabilities as well as further your own professional development
- include them in any adult social activity generated by your classroom staff, make them "family"

2) Think about how frequently you would want to have team meetings with all individuals involved with a child with disabilities. What will influence your decision as to frequency? Who do you think will be in charge of organizing and calling the meetings? Discuss your plan with another member of the class comparing decisions and discussing rationales.
- children who work with several specialists could have monthly or bi-monthly meetings to coordinate all therapies and update progress on identified objectives
- children with minor disabilities could have a mid-point progress meeting to think ahead as to what new issues need to be discussed at the PPT

- special education liaison/coordinator should call and organize the meetings but anyone can request one

3) Problem: You have never included a child with disabilities before this year. Now that you have a child with disabilities, you also find yourself with a complement of specialists as well. You are aware of the role of each type of specialist but do not understand all the language and details of therapy goals. With another class member, brainstorm several ways in which you may gain the necessary expertise you need in order to gain the maximum possible from the situation.
- ask the therapists to make brief presentations to your staff about the parameters of their therapy areas
- ask the therapists for reading materials concerning the types of work they do; read and summarize for others
- contact institutions of higher education with training programs for these therapies and request information about the field
- contact the national associations for these therapies and request basic information about the field

4) Problem: A specialist is assigned to deliver service to a child in your classroom. The therapist is new to working in applied settings having spent many years working in clinical settings. You attempt to explain the nature of your program to this person, but the specialist appears to want to proceed with business as usual. Develop a way to bring the therapist to understand the importance of what happens in your classroom.
- ask the therapist to observe the children in activity
- ask the therapist to observe the child designated for therapy within the framework of activities in the classroom and compare the level of activity, enthusiasm, and cooperation under those conditions versus the level of activity, enthusiasm, and cooperation under the condition of one-to-one therapy
- provide written information about the benefits of inclusive classrooms

5) Parents of children without disabilities need to be kept up to date concerning all the personnel they may see working within the classroom setting. Think of several ways in which you may keep parents informed while preserving the privacy of each family with a child in your room.
- look for suggestions about including information about the therapists and their specialty areas in a newsletter without identifying the specifics about why or for whom the therapists are there
- provide general information to all parents about the many types of professionals who work within the field of early childhood education

6) Some of the children in your room are curious about the children with special needs and seem to want to help them. How can you as the classroom teacher, with the support of the specialists, maximize this potential without giving the children too much responsibility?
- encourage the children to begin assisting you with simple tasks
- observe the helpers very carefully to see how well they follow through on suggestions
- observe the helpers very carefully to see how intuitive they are in their approaches to working with the children with disabilities
- observe the helpers very carefully to see how motivating they are for the children with disabilities
- help them to understand they are part of the "team"

CHAPTER 15
Observation and Assessment

1) Develop a rationale for observation as assessment for an early childhood program. The rationale will be used in a parent handbook to explain the process of observation versus other more traditional means of assessment that parents may be more familiar with. Look for suggestions that indicate that:
- observation is on-going assessment
- observation takes into account the whole child
- observation cuts across activities, skills, and different aspects of the classroom program
- observation does not take children away from learning opportunities, it is done while children are engaged in activity

2) Problem: A parent asks for an appointment with you to find out how his child is doing. You begin the meeting by asking the parent how he thinks the child is doing. The parent seems to be bothered by this line of questioning. What can you do to remedy the situation with the parent and how can you get the parent to understand that he has considerable information about the child which can add to the information you are gathering?
- look for discussion concerning the fact that while you as the teacher may know a lot about the child in terms of classroom behavior and performance, you do not know anything about the child as a member of a family, a person in a neighborhood, etc.
- encourage the parent to think of himself as an "expert" about his child
- tell the parent that you were interested in his ideas about indicators of progress
- reassure the parent that you were not trying to put him on the spot but are really interested in what he has to say

3) Think about the various forms of assessment available. Discuss the pros and cons of each of these approaches with a member of your class.
- Look for discussion about the various observation techniques in the chapter including anecdotal records, running records, event recording, duration recording, interval recording, and latency recording
- evaluation of permanent products
- rating scales
- checklists
- portfolios of various kinds
- interviews
- look for indicators of discussion on different forms of assessment such as dynamic assessment, authentic assessment, direct or performance assessment, criterion assessment, arena assessment, play based assessment, multidisciplinary assessment, interdisciplinary assessment, and transdisciplinary assessment

4) Problem: The community you are in has conducted traditional standardized assessments over the years. Recently, a committee of concerned teachers came together and determined to change the way assessments are conducted on children from preschool to third grade. You have joined the committee as a student member. What issues would you want the committee to look at in considering undertaking this major change.

- educating parents about the nature of the change, their role in the process, and the outcome of the change
- educating all teachers, paraprofessionals, and specialists about the benefits of the change
- educating the board of education
- making the assessment an ongoing part of the curriculum, not an "add on"

5) Problem: The principal of your school has asked you to serve on a committee to develop a design for portfolio assessment for the early childhood grades. If the use of portfolios is deemed appropriate and beneficial after a period of two years, other grades will join the effort. With a classmate, brainstorm a list of ideas for the types of things that may be included in the portfolio. Things that might be discussed:
- teacher observations
- written work: language arts, math, social studies, science
- art work
- other permanent products
- works in progress
- brainstormings
- journals
- audiotape language samples
- videotaped performance assessments

6) Problem: A parent comes to you and asks you how her child is doing compared to other children in the class. How will you respond to this parent? Look for discussion concerning:
- individual assessment
- child compared to self
- developmental versus chronological age
- developmental progress
- variability in skills and development of all children at this age
- variability of ability across developmental and content areas

DELMAR PUBLISHERS

ISBN 0-8273-6705-8

INSTRUCTOR'S MANUAL TO ACCOMPANY

The Developmentally Appropriate Inclusive Classroom

IN EARLY EDUCATION

Regina Miller

NOTICE TO THE READER

Publisher does not warrant or guarantee any of the products described herein or perform any independent analysis in connection with any of the product information herein. Publisher does not assume, and expressly disclaims, any obligation to obtain and include information other than that provided to it by the manufacturer.

The reader is expressly warned to consider and adopt all safety precautions that might be indicated by the activities herein and to avoid all potential hazards. By following the instructions contained herein, the reader willingly assumes all risks in connection with such instructions.

The publisher makes no representations or warranties of any kind, including but not limited to, the warranties of fitness for particular purpose or merchantability, nor are any such representations implied with respect to the material set forth herein, and the publisher takes no responsibility with respect to such material. The publisher shall not be liable for any special, consequential or exemplary damages resulting, in whole or in part, from the readers' use of, or reliance upon, this material.

COPYRIGHT © 1996
By Delmar Publishers
A division of International Thomson Publishing Inc.

The ITP logo is a trademark under license

Printed in the United States of America

For more information, contact:

Delmar Publishers
3 Columbia Circle, Box 15015
Albany, New York 12212-5015

International Thomson Publishing Europe
Berkshire House 168-173
High Holborn
London, WC1V7AA
England

Thomas Nelson Australia
102 Dodds Street
South Melbourne, 3205
Victoria, Australia

Nelson Canada
1120 Birchmount Road
Scarborough, Ontario
Canada M1K 5G4

International Thomson Editores
Campos Eliseos 385, Piso 7
Col Polanco
11560 Mexico D F Mexico

International Thomson Publishing GmbH
Königswinterer Strasse 418
53227 Bonn
Germany

International Thomson Publishing Asia
221 Henderson Road
#05-10 Henderson Building
Singapore 0315

International Thomson Publishing—Japan
Hirakawacho Kyowa Building, 3F
2-2-1 Hirakawacho
Chiyoda-ku, Tokyo 102
Japan

All rights reserved. No part of this work covered by the copyright hereon may be reproduced or used in any form or by any means—graphic, electronic, or mechanical, including photocopying, recording, taping, or information storage and retrieval systems—without the written permission of the publisher.
1 2 3 4 5 6 7 8 9 10 XXX 01 00 99 98 97 96 95

ISBN 0-8273-6705-8

Library of Congress Catalog Card Number: 95-13337